I'm a Leader!
Now What Do I Do?

50 Real Tips and Tricks for New Leaders

Stephen P. Jones

ISBN: 1523686294
ISBN-13: 978-1523686292

DEDICATION

To my wife, Christina, and my children, Madison, London, and Grayson, who all lead me far more than I lead them. You are the reason I work, you are the reason I love, you are the reason I strive to be better.

ACKNOWLEDGMENTS

To all of those I've had the honor of leading, thank you for allowing me that honor and for being patient as I, too, am always learning.

To all of those that have led me, thank you for modeling the way. Sometimes I've learned what to do and sometimes I've learned what not to do. I only hope I lead more with the former and not the latter.

Special thanks to my mother, Shirley, who reminded me to never stop identifying and achieving dreams, regardless of age or circumstance. Thanks also to my step-father, Randy, now author R.K. Walker, who inspired me to be proud of the words I put on paper.

Foreword

Leading people is a calling. It is an honor. It means that you are not only responsible for your income and the needs of yourself and your family; you now have a responsibility to those that work for you. Their wellbeing is very much influenced and in many ways dependent on your leadership. You have a lot of responsibility.

Additionally, the skill of leadership is one that transcends industry and function. It is a skill that will always serve you better the more you develop it. You may possess natural leadership ability. Perhaps you always seem to find yourself elevated to a direction giving role. Perhaps not. Regardless, leadership can be learned. Pitfalls can be avoided and you can be an effective leader.

There are a million leadership books out there. I know, I've read many of them. I've found some inspiring, pushing me to find ways to really lead better. I've found some incredibly boring, practically putting me to sleep. Mostly, I've found them to be extremely repetitive. The truth is, in this day and age, if you want to write a successful book on business, you have to learn how to take a topic and draw it out for hundreds of pages. This is not that book.

I also realized that many books were very… high level. That is to say, authors would tell this overarching strategy like "Take Risks" or "Follow Your Passion" or my personal favorite, "Never Settle". Now, don't get me wrong, all of these things are great advice. Truly, I hope you take risks and follow your passion. What these types of books often fail at is the how. How can you lead your team and be a happier, more fulfilled person?

When I sat down to write what I thought would be another blog, I realized I was really passionate about real world tactical tips that I use in my own personal pursuit to be a better leader. A few tips became ten became 25 and finally became 50. Everything in this book comes from my own experience. I am no expert but I try to follow the tips laid forth in this book. Some of it may apply for you and some may not. Take it for what it's worth. Some items on this list may work better for you and some may not work at all. I provide these lessons that I learned in an attempt to help you take some real action.

I'm not a CEO. I am no millionaire. I don't have a million followers on Twitter or lucrative speaking engagements. Someday I may have all of those things. Perhaps not. What I am is a guy who really cares about the people I lead, their wellbeing, their development and their future. I hope you are the same kind of person which is what has driven you to find some real tips you can use.

This is not a long book. I did my best to be clear and concise, not to add content for no reason. Each tip is just that, a tip. A brief explanation follows including actionable steps you can take to put it into practice. The desire is to give you some quick hit knowledge that will change some of your activities and let you further develop your leadership ability.

Best wishes on your own leadership journey. Leadership is not for the faint of heart. Always be a learner, even when serving as a teacher. Stay inspired even as you are attempting to inspire. Continue listening even as you must speak direction. It's a wild and rewarding ride worth taking. Good luck and happy reading.

Lead Happier. Be Happier.

-Stephen

1. Understand you don't have to know it all.

So, you are a new leader. You did so well that your company trusted you to lead some people. Congratulations. Now you will learn like we all did, just because you're the boss doesn't make you any smarter. You don't magically have the answers. You may feel like you have to fake it until you make it. Don't worry, that's how you should feel. So take a breath and get ready.

Most likely this feeling of panic or overwhelming stress will pass in about 6 months. Each time this happens to me, I try to remember the last time I changed positions and how that felt. If you've only just begun your role, you are on fire to do a great job but may be struggling to determine just how to fill your time. It is OK. I promise. It is perfectly normal as you begin this leadership journey to feel unqualified or overwhelmed. I remember thinking, "How did I talk my way into this job?!?" I promise, you will get there.

If you are feeling this way right now, place a reminder on your calendar for six months from today. When it alerts you, see if you don't feel significantly better. Things may not be perfect, but I'm willing to bet you're doing a lot better than you though you would.

Actions:

- Discuss this feeling with someone you trust like a friend or spouse.

- Set a reminder in your calendar for 6 months from today to check in and see how you are feeling.

- Remind yourself of a time you felt this way and intentionally recall how you moved through it.

2. Respect the past.

If you are a new leader coming into a team, make sure you take the time to learn about the past. I can't stress this enough; don't just start changing things for the sake of change. Don't just put your fingerprint on things to let everyone know you are there and you are the boss. It makes you look foolish and arrogant.

Spend time with each associate and then meet as a team. Ask questions about what they do. Be a learner. What is the history of the team? Ask if there is anything they would change. This is not about what you think; this is about what they think.

Chances are the team had a leader before you. They may have loved that leader. They may love the work they do. There may be a real sense of fear that you, the new leader on the block, are going to come in and turn everything upside down. Don't. Take time to learn and respect the past. You really need to understand the function, culture, and history first. It will do wonders for your credibility and your relationship with the team. Then, with more complete knowledge and a unified team, you can begin transformations to enhance the business.

Action:

- Talk with your leader about the history of the team.

- Talk with each associate separately, and then meet as a team.

- Acknowledge the past successes and include your team in any changes you are considering.

3. **Dress to impress.**

You've heard the saying, "Don't dress for the job you have, dress for the job you want." Well, it's true. To a point. It is far better to be overdressed for a party than underdressed. The same can be said for work. You don't want to be in jeans when everyone else is rocking the business suit. You needn't go overboard. Today's business environment is far more casual than ever before. Depending on what you do, you don't necessarily need to speed thousands of dollars on your wardrobe. Just being slightly above your company's normal dress code will definitely enhance your own personal brand.

Take a look around your company. Is it a jeans and polo kind of place? Is it more shirt and tie? Does everyone wear a suit every day? Maybe you have a uniform or wear overalls and work boots. Whatever it is, take it up one step. If everyone is in jeans, wear khakis, slacks or a skirt. If everyone is business casual, try wearing a suit once in a while. People may ask if you have an interview, but hey, so what? Nothing wrong with taking some pride in your attire.

Action

- Identify what attire is acceptable at work.

- Look for ways to increase your professional style to rise above the norm.

- Don't abandon your own sense of style.

- Don't over-invest in clothing unless that's your personal interest.

- Shop smart and dress well to show respect for your work environment and pride in your personal appearance.

4. Get a mentor.

Remember when I said you don't have to know it all? Well, you don't. Find a mentor in or out of your company that has been at this leadership thing a bit longer than you. They don't know it all either, but they probably know more than you.

First, to find a mentor, start by talking with your own leader. Ask for suggestions. This shows a real willingness to learn, a humble nature and a desire to do better. Look at your peer team, other leaders at your same level. Select one that has been in their position at least a year. Reach out and ask if he or she would be open to providing some mentoring.

If you are struggling to find someone in your company, look into professional groups such as a chamber of commerce or a networking group. Look through your LinkedIn as well.

For leaders that have not been mentors, they may be caught off guard. Just explain you would like to leverage their knowledge so you can learn how to do your own job better. Most often, a person feels incredibly flattered to be able to play the role of teach.

Start with weekly or bi-weekly one-on-one meetings of an hour. Be ready to drive the conversation.

Some people are great at being mentors, but some aren't quite sure what you are looking for. Bring in questions and real life scenarios to get their opinion and gain insight. You can leverage strong leaders to learn how to lead difficult associates, manage tough stakeholders and gather a variety of company information.

Action

- Talk with your leader and find a suitable mentor.

- Meet weekly or bi-weekly for an hour.

- Arrive ready with specific questions, scenarios and topics to drive your own learning.

5. Redefine success.

I know I promised no high-level fluff, so let me explain. If you are a new leader, no longer does your feeling of accomplishment come from what you do. It now comes from what your team does. People may come to you for updates or to make assignments, but now, more often than not, you aren't doing the tactical work. You may be casting the vision, laying out the strategy, or inspecting the final product, but you have a team that is doing the work.

This can be a huge change, especially if you have always been a high performer. Redefine success as what your team does. If your team is kicking out great work and really driving the business foreword, you should feel incredibly proud. Their success is your success. Hold on to that feeling.

Now that doesn't mean you should take credit for work you didn't do. If you are receiving praise for work coming from your team, accept it graciously but in your response make mention of your incredible team. When praise comes in, make sure you bring it back to the team. It will build relationships and your creditability.

Action

- Keep a running list of successes and completed projects that have come from your team.

- Share this list with you leader and take pride in the successes of the team.

- Consider a "Success Wall" where people can write and share their successes.

6. Define your vision and mission together.

When starting a new team, it's important to build the right foundation. That typically comes in the form of a Vision – what we want the world to look like thanks to our team, and a Mission – how we are dedicated to getting there. If you have these things handed to you, at the very least talk about it as a team so that you understand it the same way. If you need to define these, ask your team how they feel about the work they do.

I've found the best way to accomplish this with a new team is to take a day or two to step away from the daily tasks and spend time together. Host an off-site meeting if possible. Part of this meeting should include a vision and mission exercise. Have each member write down answers to two questions:

1. If our team is doing the best we possibly can, what does our world look like?
2. What are we going to do to get us there?

If you are in sales your answers may look like, "We are exceeding our sales goals each month and leading the company in customer engagement," and, "We are dedicated to treating each customer like family to ensure we grow the business and exceed our goals each month."

This is something you should be able to point back to and say, "How are the activities we are doing today supporting our mission and vision?" If they aren't, you need to ask yourself if you are doing the right activities or if you still have the right vision and mission.

Action

- Set up a one or two day meeting off site, if possible.

- Take your team through the Vision and Mission exercise.

- Consider providing colored pencils and sketch paper to encourage creativity.

- Work to answer the referenced questions.

- Work as a team to wordsmith the final product.

7. Define your annual goals together.

You did your Vision and Mission, right? Great. Now, what are the specifics the team will focus on to bring those things to life? Work as a team to have a conversation about goals. You want to be able to look back at the end of the year and say, "Yep, we hit those goals out of the park!"

In that offsite meeting you are hosting, spend some time as a team working on goals. Start with your company priorities if they have been outlined. How do your goals align with those? Failure to align goals with you company could mean you won't get the support from other areas of the business. It may also keep you from meeting the expectations of your own leader.

When setting goals, I say don't set more than five. A goal should be high level with specific actions below it. For instance, if the goal is to meet your sales quota, your specific actions may be to consistently cold call, follow up within 24 hours and always send thank you cards.

Make your goals SMART:

- Specific
- Meaningful
- Action Oriented
- Realistic
- Timely

I didn't invent this, but I use the heck out of it.

Action

- On a white board or sketch pad, outline the company's goals or priorities.

- Section each off and lead a group dialogue around how your team can impact each area.

- Agree on two or three activities under each and document them.

- Make sure your goals also reflect the Vision and Mission of your team.

8. Schedule one-on-ones, and keep them.

Many of those I have lead in the past would chuckle at reading this. Keeping one on one meetings is harder than you might think. But, growing your team means growing your people. The first step is to develop a relationship. To provide leadership, you have to have a relationship.

Schedule a one hour weekly one-on-one meeting with each person on your team. The larger the team, the more difficult this may be. In the beginning, however, it is foundational. As time goes on, you may be able to move to a bi-weekly or even monthly one-on-ones. You may be able to scale back to 30 minutes.

If possible, have these meetings in person. Come prepared to drive the meeting foreword. Some associates will fill the time easily, while others will struggle with what to discuss. I like to start with their list. "Do you have anything on your list for me?" is my first question. If they struggle, redirect. Ask for updates on specific projects. Anything positive or negative happening that comes to mind? Take notes so that you can refer back to them in following one on ones. This let's your associate know that you care enough to keep up with what's on their plate.

Lastly, this time is sacred and if canceled should be rescheduled. This is harder than it sounds, especially if you have a large team and work in a meeting driven environment. You and your associates will get double booked and finding make up time is difficult. Make it a priority and don't beat yourself up if you miss one. Just do better.

Action

- Open your calendar and create a recurring one hour meeting for each of your associates.

- Find time that works for you and for them.

- Set a clear expectation in the body that this is "their time" but you would like to know about any business updates, new work begun and anything they need to be successful.

9. Host a weekly meeting.

I know that no one likes the Monday morning meeting. Actually, I do like it. I may be the only one. But, that said, you need to get your team together on a regular basis to instill the value of team approach. Spending time together develops trust and respect that will be very important.

Make sure your meeting has purpose. No one likes to go to a meaningless meeting. On top of that, consider all the blogs and articles that talk about how much time we waste in meetings. Don't contribute to that mess. Make sure you have a plan.

I like to start each meeting with an activity to let the team get to know each other personally. I provide the team any assignments or company news that I need to share. We then move to updates and each associate comes with a summary of what they are working on. This keeps the team connected. Nothing is worse than someone saying, "I didn't know you were working on that!"

Just like one on ones, team meetings should be considered sacred. Never cancel if you can help it.

Action

- Open your calendar and create a one hour minimum recurring weekly meeting.
- Determine the day and time that works best for all of your team.
- Include an agenda in the invitation that will be followed each week.
- The agenda should include:
    - Team Building (Relationship Building)
    - Leader Updates
    - New Work Assignments
    - Team Updates
    - Special Guest (when applicable)
    - Round Table

10. Play Rose and Thorn.

As I was looking for ways to engage my children at the dinner table, I came across this game called Rose and Thorn. You may have heard it called Highs and Lows. If you have children, you may be familiar with the universal answer to the question, "How was your day?" Fine. The answer is always fine. Rose and Thorn provides a little more detail.

Here are the rules:

A rose is something that went really well during the day. A thorn is something that was challenging.

During that meeting with purpose you host weekly, begin with Rose and Thorn for the team building portion. Ask everyone to share a rose and a thorn. It may be personal or professional. Associates should only share what they are comfortable sharing. This is a great way to know more about your team and for your team to build those personal relationships.

You may feel this is a bit silly, but spending time learning about what's important to people inside or outside of work builds stronger relationships within the team. You want a team that truly cares about each other and their wellbeing.

Action

- Explain that to start each meeting, so that you all can continue learning about each other and stay up to date, you will play a game.

- Outline the game and make sure associates know they only should share what they are comfortable sharing.

- Go first to show your team how the game works.

- As each person goes, allow them to choose the next person.

11. Make your workplace fun.

People can't work eight hours straight through. In fact, the whole eight hour work day is outdated. There is a way get better productivity and have happier associates. Make work fun.

A better way to work is to focus for about an hour but then step away for 15 minutes. This actually gives you more productivity and a better work product. The key is to make your workplace fun so there is something fun to step away to do. Depending on your company and your culture, this may look different.

We have a common table with a puzzle and other little toys. When the team needs a break they work on the puzzle for a few minutes. It promotes team work and gives their mind a break from work.

If you work for a company that creates a fun work environment then I am envious. But for those of us who don't work for companies like Google, Apple or Zappos, I suggest small changes. Keep things like stress toys, silly putty, mind bender puzzles and slinkies. Try to provide something to keep the mind going. Anything you can do to brighten the work environment up will have a positive impact on your team.

Action

- Find a common area you can designate as a recharge area.

- Hit the dollar store or discount store and pick up some small stress relieving toys.

- Encourage associate to bring items as well.

- Encourage use of the area by modeling the way and using it too.

12. Send thank you cards.

Personalized handwritten thank you cards are a thing of the past. Taking the time to actually write one means so much. It's such a small thing but so overlooked in the days of emails, instant messages, texts and tweets. Consider the last time you received a thank you card and how it made you feel.

Try to send a thank you card at least once a week. Send one to people on your team or someone with whom you worked. Be specific in your words as to why you are thankful. Be genuine. Be appreciative for those that take the time to help further your own work. This is a great way to enhance relationships and your own personal brand. Being known as thoughtful and thankful surely can't hurt.

Action

- Buy Thank You cards in bulk so you always have them on hand.

- Set a reminder in your calendar for once a week.

- Be specific in your message of appreciation.

13. Remember birthdays and anniversaries.

Take time to remember important dates like birthdays and anniversaries. Put them in your calendar with a reminder a few days in advance. Bring donuts or bagels and circulate the greeting card. Take the lead from what other leaders do in your company. We print birthday signs and decorate cubicles. It may seem a bit childish, but everyone likes to have a day dedicated to them.

Plus, there is nothing more embarrassing than to show up and be the last to know it's someone's birthday or anniversary, especially if that person is on your team. Be the one that always remembers important dates and your associates will appreciate the attention to detail. It's an important way to show you care!

Action

- Place each birthday and anniversary in your calendar with a reminder three days before.

- Work with your team to execute whatever is appropriate for your company. At minimum, circulate a card.

- Always keep blank greeting cards as a precaution.

14. Buy breakfast for no reason.

Sometimes, even when it's not someone's birthday, pick up something for breakfast. Maybe a new bakery opened by the office or maybe you just happen to be running a bit early on the way to work. Grab a dozen donuts, a box of bagels, or a fruit tray. It doesn't matter what, just bring in something to show you appreciate that people choose to wake up every morning and come spend it working with you.

Little things like this continue to show you care. I'm not saying do it every day or even once a week, but on occasion, grab some breakfast.

Action

- Take note of what bakeries, bagel shops, donut shops and grocery stores you pass on your way to work.

- Make it a point to bring in breakfast once a quarter.

- Try to include a variety to respect those with allergies or attempting to eat healthy.

15. Remember recognition.

Recognition goes a long way. Think about how you feel when someone recognizes you for your work. Great, right? You feel appreciated and valued. Isn't that exactly how you want your team to feel? Take the time to recognize associates for the great things they do.

Some companies have formal methods for recognition such as award nominations or just little emailed forms of appreciation. Use formal methods if available. Also, use informal methods such as showing appreciation during a team meeting or sending an informal email.

Make sure you spread the praise around. No one feels good when they feel like the boss is playing favorites. Look for the successes from all the members of your team. Also, encourage your people to recognize each other. Peer to peer recognition is a great way to grow the culture of the team.

Learn how people on your team like to be recognized. Some may be embarrassed to be the center of attention while others enjoy the grand event. Recognition is about the recipient first.

Action

- List successes gathered from your one on ones and weekly meetings.

- If available, use formal methods of recognition such as award nominations.

- Use informal methods such as meeting recognition or emails.

- Encourage peer to peer recognition.

16. Celebrate the wins!

Did you just finish a great project? Did you just meet your sales goal? Did something great happen? Too often we have a checkbox mentality. We finish one task and we are on to the next. We spend so much time working towards the goal that we forget to celebrate when we achieve it. Take a moment and recognize the work you do and the things you accomplish.

Take off early and go buy a round of drinks in celebration. Have the team recognized at the company wide meeting. Just take a moment and acknowledge a milestone in team accomplishment.

Action

- Document large team successes in your weekly meeting.

- Identify ways in which you can celebrate.

- Do so no less than once a quarter.

17. Career path your people.

Your associates will not be your associates forever. Just like you have moved positions, your associates deserve their next step. You have an obligation to develop your associates into their next promotion.

In those one on ones you have to ask this question, "What's next?" I know you never want to think about anybody leaving. Why would anyone want to leave your amazing leadership? But failing to support and career path people will cause turnover even more quickly. You're number one job is to get your people ready for their next step – if they want a next step. Why is that your number one? People who are challenged are learning to be better. When you get better, you become a high performer. You want to create and encourage high performers. High performers get promoted.

Think about the best leaders you've had in your journey. I'll bet they were the ones that taught you, inspired you and helped you achieve your next step along the way. Be that leader for your people.

Action

- In your one on one meeting, ask your associate where they see their next step.

- Provide growth opportunities through stretch assignments or shadowing.

- Assist in finding your associate a mentor that can help towards that next step.

18.Encourage work life balance.

There is no faster way to increase turnover than to ignore work life balance. You and all of your associates may love to work. You may love to work all the time. I wish you that type of joy. Even so, you are not your job. You deserve time to disconnect and recharge by engaging in activities you like to do.

Now that you are a leader, you are managing more than your own work life balance. You are managing your team's as well. Of course, your company may expect 40 hours, or 50 or 60 for that matter. But if that is not your expectation, you need to make it known.

Everyone's work life balance is different. As a leader of a team, you need to be cognizant of people's work life balance. Set expectations as to when you expect people to be at work or available, and when you don't. Time off is time off and failure to respect that can lead to burn out. If you need people on call, try to rotate the responsibility so that people can truly disconnect from work.

Respect vacation days and encourage associates to use benefit time. That is what it's there for. Give your associates permission to disconnect and be weary of comments made in jest. If an associate comes in later than usual, the comment, "Thanks for gracing us with your presence," while funny in your own mind, has a serious weight coming from a leader to an associate.

Action

- Set clear expectations as to the core hours you want associates to be present.

- Explain that benefit time is important and should be used.

- Respect when associates are off work.

from a leader to an associate.

Action

- Set clear expectations as to the core hours you want associates to be present.

- Explain that benefit time is important and should be used.

- Respect when associates are off work.

19. Watch your own time.

As a leader, your team is watching you. You are modeling the way and inadvertently encouraging your associates with every action you take. If you constantly show up an hour before everyone else or stay late most nights, your team may think that's your expectation. They may try to mirror you. You will burn them out. If that's not your expectation, you'd better make it known.

You need work life balance too. If you are coming in early and staying late, you could burn out. An overworked stressed out leader is not effective. If you aren't able to maintain work life balance, you need to examine your own activities and responsibilities.

On the other hand, if you are constantly arriving late or leaving early, you will lose the respect of your team. Plan your time off and make sure you inform your team. If you must take a day off or leave early, let your team know. You never want to be known as the absentee leader.

Action

- Set clear expectations as to when your team can expect to find you working.

- Be clear about your expectations of the team's availability.

- Be dependable and consistent.

- Keep your team informed of any changes to your availability.

20. Understand sick time.

Oh, sick time. That benefit you feel like you shouldn't use for fear of being labeled the abuser. You will have associates that never call in sick. You will have associates that always call in sick. You may feel like you can never call in sick because you have to lead by example. Managing sick time, or really all benefit time, is one of those less than fun parts about leading people.

Specific to sick time, however, give the benefit of the doubt. Do this for a couple of reasons. First, you want to be understanding and supportive of your team. Sometimes people are sick. It's life. They don't feel good. You certainly don't want to be anything less than supportive when someone is already feeling terrible. You want to be a leader who cares about your team. You want to show trust and respect and not create fear or resentment. Remember the values you are instilling in your team.

Second, you don't want more sick people. You want people to stay home and get well. This goes for you too. The world will not end. The company will not crumble without your presence. If you come to work sick, you are modeling the way that you expect your associates to come to work sick. Additionally, you are putting everyone in the office at risk.

Read your HR policy and make sure your team knows it. If you company requires a doctors not then get a doctor's note.

If it's up to you, be lenient and understanding. Give people the benefit of the doubt. If you uncover a significant trend of abuse, then address it.

Action

- Understand benefit time and policies around the use of sick time.

- Be supportive and understanding to those that must use sick time.

- Don't come to work sick.

- Educate your associates on the HR policies to ensure they are taking appropriate action as needed.

21. Be a cheerleader.

A cheerleader encourages the players. They dedicate their energy to the success of the team they support. Their victory comes with the victory of the team. In addition, they hype up the crowd to do the same. In essence, their happiness comes at the success of their team. See the correlation?

It's time to cheer on your players. It's time to tell your team how proud you are of what is being accomplished and reinforce that you know they can do it, whatever it equates to in your world. It's time to get your happiness from your team's success. Then tell everyone else around you. Tell your peer leadership team. If a forum to share doesn't exist, create one in which you and other leaders can highlight major initiatives.

Lastly, make sure you cheer on your associates up to your own leader. Let your organizational leadership know of major milestones and successes. Express your pride and faith in your associates and the work they do. You should be a conduit of praise from your leader to each and every associate on your team.

Action

- Keep notes on all projects and work efforts coming from your team.

- Use encouraging words in team meetings and one on ones.

- Share successes with other teams and your leader on a consistent basis.

- If no good forum exists, propose a biweekly cross-functional engagement meeting where associates can present projects they are leading.

22. Be a quarterback.

A quarterback calls the plays. But once the play is called, he relies on the team to execute. You can't do this all by yourself, so don't even try. Look at your work, make the play call, and trust your team to execute.

A quarterback sees the whole field in order to make the appropriate decisions to win the game. A quarterback gives the ball to the right player. When the game is won, a good quarterback gives the glory to his team.

Enough football references for you? Just remember this, trust your own leader and your organization as your coach, call your plays and let the team run them to succeed.

Action

- When faced with a new task, determine who on your team is best suited or who could benefit most from the experience.

- Outline the project; explain the desired outcome and the timeline.

- Trust your associate to execute but be available for guidance.

23. Inspect the culture of the team.

The culture of your team should never be a surprise. Use deliberate language to let your team know how important team culture is to you. If your company provides culture direction, use it. If not, consider the behaviors you want your team to display. Use terms like "respect", "team approach", and "trust" often.

In both your team meetings and your one on ones, make sure you are asking, "How are you?" and, "How's the team?" Listen for any concerns, heightened levels of stress or frustration with anyone or anything. You can't expect work to be sunshine and rainbows all the time but you never want to be surprised by any problems with your team culture.

Action

- Use deliberate words that describe the values you want your team to possess.

- In every one on one, make time to talk about how the associate is feeling about work and the team.

- In team meetings, make time for culture activities such as asking associates to provide recent examples that embody a value like "respect" or "trust".

24. Resolve team conflict.

At some point, your associates are going to fight amongst themselves. It is going to happen. Teams are made up of people and people don't always get along. Then, they will look at you like, "What are you going to do about it?"

You can be the leader that ignores or sweeps problems under the rug, but I don't recommend it. I recommend you be the leader that leads through conflict. Get comfortable with the uncomfortable, tough conversations.

Team conflict must be addressed swiftly. Rifts in a team can turn toxic quickly. Many times, you may not even realize there is an issue until it's too late. Leverage your relationships to continue understanding your team dynamic so you are not caught off guard. If a disagreement, or worse, a personality conflict arises, bring in the people and talk through it. If at all possible, come to an understanding without placing blame. Let all parties know they may respectfully disagree. The key word is respectfully.

You want to build team approach and trust. Make sure this is known. Continue to meet with each person individually to provide guidance and coaching while ensuring you keep informed of any future problems.

Action

- Uncover problems through consistent one on ones and team meetings.

- Once identified, deal with problems swiftly by mediating meaningful conversations between associates.

- Set expectations about respect, how the team works together and how they treat each other.

25. Give opportunities to stretch.

You have an obligation to grow your associates. They need a chance to shine. If you aren't creating those opportunities, you are not only doing a disservice to your people, you are doing a disservice to yourself. The success of a leader is the success of the team. There is no greater success than developing your associates.

Once upon a time, you were given an opportunity to do something you had never done. You had no idea what you were doing but, somehow, you made it through. Look for those opportunities for your team. Can someone drive a project, lead a meeting or represent you and your team on a high impact initiative? They may not have done it exactly the way you would have or as good as you could have. They may fail. Regardless, you just gave them trust, empowerment, and the ability do something they have never done before.

Stretch assignments are also a great tool when thinking about their career path. If your associate has defined their desired next step, find stretch assignments that let them improve knowledge and relationships in that area.

Be there to support and offer guidance but remember to let them have their time to experience and ultimately succeed.

Action

- Examine your responsibilities and determine if an associate could stretch into accepting something you currently do.

- Work with other leaders to identify stretch opportunities to grow associates in new functions.

- For those looking at leadership, look for temporary assignments that may involve directly or indirectly leading people.

26. Teach personal brand.

Personal brand is one of the most difficult conversations to have because personal brand is, well, personal. Personal brand is how people see you, how you show up at work, and what you stand for. If one of your associates comes up in conversation, what are the first three words someone would use to describe them? Are they reliable, fun, and innovative? Or would people say they are argumentative, arrogant, or rude?

Personal brand is the difference between someone saying, "Oh, I love working with that guy," and "Oh, I hate working with that guy." Or worse yet, "Who is that guy?"

Many people believe their merit should stand on the quality of their work. That's true and it should. But it doesn't, at least not all by itself. Let's say the perfect position comes open for one of your people. You want that hiring manager to not only know who your associate is, but also why they are a great candidate. And that comes from personal brand.

Talk about this often to encourage the concept of being known for something positive. Be a brand advocate for your people. Talk about their strengths and showcase their talents. Talk to other leaders about your associate's career path and where they would like to go. Then, when that opportunity arises, people will be expecting that move.

Action

- Explain to your team why personal brand is important.

- Take your team through a personal brand exercise asking them what they want to be known for. Start with:

  o When working with me, I want others to feel…

  o I want to be known for…

- If you are made aware that an associate has a poor personal brand, have a one-on-one conversation with your associate and specifically call out what actions have led to a potential negative impression.

- Model the way by ensuring you are aware and managing your own personal brand.

27. Take time to learn.

Never stop learning. This has been my mantra since high school. In order to remain effective as a leader, you need to take time for personal development. I don't mean checking out a couple of LinkedIn blogs – though you should do that too. I mean real educational development. This will keep you sharp on whatever functional area you lead such as sales, marketing or operations. It will also keep you bringing a fresh and innovative perspective.

Finding leadership development will keep you engaged with your team and looking for new and better ways to develop each of your associates. Being able to contribute new approaches and thinking inspires a team.

If you work for a company that encourages learning, find seminars, conferences, and classes. Step away from the business to learn. Truly disconnect form work and focus on the development.

If you don't have the budget for such things, look for free online learnings. There are some incredible resources available. Make sure you document all learnings and leverage them in your work. It will not only feel good to improve yourself; your own leader will appreciate you took the initiative.

Action

- In your goals, document one or two areas you would like to develop.

- Identify if formal learning opportunities are available and discuss with your leader.

- Look for ways to learn from experts in blogs, tweets and other posts.

- Consider additional resources such as books or audiobooks at your local library. Find online resources that offer free and inexpensive programs. Try:

    o Coursera.com

    o Lynda.com

    o Edx.com

28. Teach office politics.

I know "office politics" sounds like a bad word. I believe it's how you define it. If you think of office politics as an unethical, favor trading, favorite having, boys (or girls) club environment, I would agree. Never lose your ethics and hurt people to further yourself. I don't care what industry you find yourself in, I believe those type of leaders are short-lived.

Office politics is the not so great word for "we like to work with people we like." I think of office politics as taking time to build relationships with those you work with and depend on for the sake of the business. Done right, office politics is really more about respect and relationship building. Taking time, making the effort, and identifying the best partners in your company saves you time, frustration, and increases the quality of your work.

It's a fact of life that relationships get work done. Teach your associates to build relationships whenever they can. This is where the personal brand work will also compliment. Just like you need to nurture relationships, you're associate do, too.

Action

- Talk with your associates about the importance of cross-functional relationships.

- Encourage your associates to set up a one on ones monthly with someone they don't know to create new relationships.

- Invite other groups to your meeting to explain more about their area of the business.

29. Study your whole company.

You play a piece of a larger whole. Get out the org chart, the company vision and mission. Locate anything else that can help you see the bigger picture such as cultural documents or initiative information.

The higher you climb on the leadership ladder, the larger a view you need of the company. Having knowledge of why things are the way they are or how things work will give you an advantage as you tackle your own work. As a leader, your team needs to be able to look to you for strategic guidance. The better you understand the company, the better you can maximize the part your team plays.

Set meetings with leaders of other functions to better understand how things work together. This not only gives you an opportunity to learn more about the company, this also is a great time to share your team responsibilities.

Action

- Access your organizational chart or structure.

- Note the breakdown of functional area and learn the senior leaders in each.

- Continue working down the org chart to learn about the detailed areas that exist.

- Use all other information such as the Vision, the Mission, cultural information and major initiatives to help fuel your research.

- Meet with other leaders to learn more about their area of the business.

30. Explain the power of social for business.

Today, the power of social for business is synonymous with LinkedIn. But, just as once upon a time, social meant Myspace, (what's Myspace?), the future of social for business is ever expanding. Social for business is a more all-encompassing term that covers blogs, forums, streams and relationships that can occur for the sake of business. Basically, unless you specifically renounced all things online, or only recently were rescued from a desert island, you know that social for business is big and you are probably already participating in it.

First, start with the obvious. If you don't have a LinkedIn account, get one. It will let you connect with colleagues in your industry and gives you access to some great information. Second, encourage, but don't mandate, that associates have an updated LinkedIn profile. It's just good to keep up with your own experience and resume and having this updated profile allows others to easily learn about you.

I use links to LinkedIn profiles in Organizational Announcements (when someone is hired or promoted) and also in the signature of my own emails. I encourage you and your associates to do the same. You'll never know when a contact can come in handy.

Explain the importance of professionalism online. This is not only for LinkedIn but across all open social platforms. While

I don't recommend you social stalk your associates, you never want to put something out there that you would be embarrassed for your leader to see. Someone taught me a long time ago never to do something that makes people not want to do business with you. That is, unless you don't want to do business with them.

I'd also like to point out that professionalism does not negate fun. For you and your associates, it is your own social world and you should feel free to share what you want. Some platforms are dedicated to business, some for personal and some for both. Pictures of dogs, babies, your favorite craft beer or your favorite sports team; it's up to you what you want to put out to the universe. My recommendation is to always keep it positive. Either limit the viewing audience, or consider the reaction your content might create and how you feel about that fact.

Action

- Create and keep updated a LinkedIn profile. Encourage but don't require associates do the same.

- Incorporate LinkedIn profile links where appropriate.

- Be cognizant of your own online brand.

- Teach the importance of online brand awareness to your team.

- Look for other business social sites specific to your geographic or functional area.

31.Explain the bigger picture.

It's easy to only see the work right in front of your face. It's right there, every day, in your face. It may be more difficult to see how the work you do contributes to the success of the larger organization. Now that you have a better understanding of your whole company, you should be able to understand how the work you do contributes to the larger goal.

You have to take that information to your team. Failing to feel connected to a larger vision and see your importance is one of the main reasons people leave a company.

Look at what your team does for the sake of the company. If you didn't exist, what might happen? Talk through the importance of the work they do and explain how they are connected. Draw a path to the other teams you affect. If your team doesn't meet a deadline, how does that affect other teams around you? If another team is covered up in work, how are you impacted?

Understanding how interdependent all teams are in your company can promote a larger team approach mentality. New relationships will grow, partnerships formed, and work accomplished.

Action

- In a team meeting, draw the high level org chart on a white board and talk about who leads each area and how it contributes to the company.

- Ask associates to talk about how what they do impacts the company.

- Ask each associate to take one area of the business and do a deep dive to understand what the smaller teams do.

- Have associates teach back what they learned.

32. Be transparent and collaborate.

This is a big one. You have a team of highly capable experts that want to do amazing work. It is up to you to use them. We've already talked a lot about respect and team approach. Consider those values as you lead your team.

No one likes to feel disconnected, uninformed, or in the dark when it comes to things that affect their job. As a leader, you may participate in projects or have access to sensitive information that impacts your team.

If you can, share. Share early, share often, gather feedback, and collaborate. You may feel like you are protecting your team by not involving them for whatever reason, but you are not. In fact, if there are rumors and whispers of new projects, organizational changes, or other business impacting information, the swirl they are feeling of not knowing is killing your culture.

There will be times when you, as a leader, must keep information confidential. If this is the case, by all means, do so. But, more often than not, you are well within your right to share and collaborate with your team. Failure to do so breaks down trust and respect.

Ask yourself why you are hoarding information? Is it so you can have the power? So you can be the hero? Because you don't trust your team? This approach damages your own personal brand, breaks down your team and ultimately, makes you fail.

Action

- When necessary, work with your own leader to determine when you can share information.

- When considering what to share, consider:

    o Am I allowed to share this information?

    o Could my team provide value?

    o Will sharing promote trust and respect?

- Share with the team as a whole so no one feels excluded.

- Make the meeting a safe place to gather real reactions. Let associates process and work through their change cycle.

- Collaborate and use the feedback to better shape the situation.

33. Set clear priorities.

Nothing is more frustrating than not knowing what you should do. Now that you're the leader, it's your job to figure out what people should do. That's right; you have to cast a vision.

Before you can set clear priorities, you need to understand what the most important tasks are at hand. In a world where everything is important, nothing is important. Outline the roles and responsibilities that fall in your scope of work. Consider things like impact on the business, the customer and the bottom line first. Re-examine your vision and mission if necessary. As you look at each task ask yourself if doing it is bringing you closer to that vision. Those are your priorities, the ones that keep you in business and drive you toward the vision you said was your perfect world.

Once you are comfortable with your priorities, have an open dialogue with your team. Be open to feedback and come to an agreement on team priorities. No one likes to have assignments dictated. Make sure your team has a voice in decisions that affect their job.

Action

- Outline all roles and responsibilities and rank them in order of importance to the company, the team and the vision.

- Discuss the prioritization to the team, revise as necessary.

- Be clear in what you expect and outline what exceeding your expectations looks like.

34. Delegate appropriately and evenly.

You can't do it all on your own. That is why you lead people, because your company trusts you to do more than you can possibly do on your own. It is for this reason you must get comfortable with not being the actual doer of the work. You must get comfortable with delegation.

There are two reasons that delegation is so important. First, failure to delegate will burn you out. You will find yourself working unreasonable hours and managing an unmanageable workload. Eventually, you are going to fail, damaging your career and your personal brand.

The second reason to delegate is for the sake of your team. If you don't delegate work load you, won't be challenging your team. Your team will grow bored and complacent. When your people don't feel like they are contributing; like they are valuable, they will leave. If you aren't appropriately delegating, you are failing your team.

Finally, when it comes to delegation, do so evenly. If you have multiple tasks, responsibilities and projects, make sure you are inspecting bandwidth and disperse the workload evenly. Failure to so do will leave some feeling overwhelmed while others feel untrusted.

Action

- List out all daily responsibilities, work assignments and upcoming projects.

- Determine which tasks can be delegating and how much bandwidth each will take.

- Discuss assignments in one on ones and team meetings.

- Make sure you divide evenly.

35. Trust, empower, and inspect.

Now that the priorities are clear, step back and trust. You know you need to redefine success as the success of your team. That can make it difficult to take a more hands off approach. But that is why you have a team, so that you can execute even more for your company. If you delegate work but constantly bombard your people with questions, suggestions or worse, commands, you aren't trusting in your team or their abilities.

Remember that feeling when someone believed in you and trusted you? That's the feeling you need to give to your team. Becoming a micromanager might seem attractive, but it's a sure way to decrease your culture and burn you out.

Associates say that their happiness is dependent on their immediate leader, their ability to work autonomously and their contribution to the larger goal. That means you, just by showing trust and empowerment, can have the greatest impact on your associates cultural outlook at work.

Inspect work along the way with a respectful approach. If you find a project is not on track or a poor decision was made, coach through it, explaining how to overcome the set back and continue towards the end goal. If work continues to suffer, recognize the trend and then, and only then, pull back the empowerment.

Actions

- Trust your team to execute the work that needs to be done.

- Empower your team to make decisions. If they seek consult, provide guidance but reinforce that they have the power to make the decision as they see fit.

- Inspect work progress in team meetings and through one on ones.

- Use the right language or trust and empowerment to show your confidence in your team.

36. Let them fail.

You may be tempted to come to the rescue or take over a project the minute something doesn't go as planned. Remember that failure is one step closure to success. For every mistake, a lesson can be learned and used the next time around. Not allowing an associate to fail robs them of a crucial development process.

Remember that one poor decision or one failed attempt is not a trend. As you may feel compelled to micromanage, you may also feel compelled to pull all trust and empowerment immediately. If you do so, you will damage the culture and development of your associates.

Have you perfectly executed every work assignment ever handed to you? I doubt it. Most likely you can look back over your career and see things you wished you'd done differently, areas that could have been better. But those failures have led you to greater success. Those failures have led you to now. This should also be the way for your team.

Provide coaching and guidance during one on ones. As mentioned before, inspect work. Intervene only if absolutely necessary. Talk about how you might do something differently next time. Remember, when someone fails, they are at their most vulnerable. Don't deplete confidence even more so.

Action

- Stay up to date on work efforts in one on ones and team meetings.

- If you identify a problem, offer guidance and coach asking:

  - "What do you think you might have done differently?"

  - "What do you think the best decision for the company and our team might be?"

  - "What would you say you learned?"

- Intervene only if absolutely necessary.

37. Be a mentor.

Are you ready for a next step? If you found a mentor and utilized them for your development, you've got a debt to pay; a leadership debt. Just as you have found someone to help you on your journey, you must find someone, not on your team, who could use your guidance.

Start with letting your leader know you'd like to be a mentor. Your leader can circulate that information at their level and potentially help connect you with someone. Also, look at your own professional groups and see if any young members might be searching.

You may find that someone approaches you. Be humble and grateful if that happens. The longer you serve in a leadership role, the more likely this will happen.

Offer to set up one hour weekly meetings. Be a sounding board, offer advice, and give a safe place for ideation, development, and frustration. Some people will come prepared to utilize the time well. Some won't know how. Be ready to ask specific questions about projects or situations to help drive the conversation forward. Don't be afraid of giving your true opinion and offering direction. That is why you are a mentor. Truly, being a mentor to someone will be just as valuable for you as it is for them.

Action

- Inform you leader you are interested in becoming a mentor.

- Once someone has been identified, set up one hour weekly meetings.

- Be ready to drive the meeting if necessary by talking about projects or situations faced.

- Be bold and offer lessons you have learned in your experience.

38. Have team lunches.

Eating together is more than just gaining nourishment. We are a species who bonds over the act of eating. This has been true for hundreds of years. Today, with your team it is no different. Team lunches strengthen relationships through conversation and social interaction. People are generally more comfortable when eating and far more willing to share. New ideas can be discussed and grown into new strategies. Stories will be shared that strengthen personal and professional relationships. You will laugh and relate with one another. And this will happen all while you step away from the business.

You can do this randomly and without planning as does happen often. Remember that some people bring their lunch, some may run errands or visit the gym, and some may even take meetings. Don't assume that people will be available on a whim to dine with you.

Additionally, don't just invite a portion of the team. Be inclusive and deliberate to ensure no one feels left own. This also means you must be considerate of things like food preferences and religious or dietary restrictions.

Hopefully you have the freedom to expense such things on occasion. Truly, it is good for the team and good for business. It is an investment.

Action

- Choose a quarterly or monthly recurring date and schedule a team lunch.

- Solicit recommendations from the team for lunch options.

- Make sure to schedule enough time to get to and from lunch without being rushed.

- If acceptable, expense the cost as a team event.

39. Give gifts – equally.

If you work for a company which allows it – small gifts can be little culture enhancers. Small tokens of appreciation can remind your team that you care. It's easy to get caught up in the day to day activities and forget to show your appreciation.

For birthdays and anniversaries, give a small gift card. You can do this on your own or go in as a team. Just make sure you're consistent so someone doesn't feel left out.

Give everyone something small around the holidays. If your team is small enough, set yourself a per-person limit and try to purchase an appropriate gift that matches their interest. This is a great way to show you care enough to know each person and their interests and that you took the time to find a gift just for them. Also consider personalized gifts that can be used around the office.

If your team is large in size you may need to set your limit lower and buy everyone the same gift. Consider buying something in bulk that relates to your team or industry. Shop smart and plan ahead to make the most of your money.

Action

- For birthdays and anniversaries, give a small gift card or go in as a team on a larger gift card.

- For the end of the year holidays, give similar value items to each team member.

- For larger teams, buy in bulk to maximize your spend.

- Always be fair and equal when giving gifts.

- Always be work appropriate when giving gifts.

40. Be thankful.

This may not feel very tactical, but it really is specific action you should take. Right now, look at where you are. Be present in this moment and recognize what you do for your company, your team, you family and yourself. You have been trusted to lead people. You are providing for yourself and possible others. You are making a significant impact to your company. Unfortunately, life sometimes moves so fast that you fail to recognize how far you've come.

Be thankful for the life you have and the work you do. Remember you are contributing to something bigger than yourself. Being able to stop and recognize the good things in your life will help you keep a positive outlook and enhance your productivity and culture at work. People like to be around happy people, and you should be happy!

Action

- Make a list of all the things for which you are thankful in your life. Include both business and personal items.

- Take 30 minutes a week minimum to read this list and dwell on this list.

- Add to this list and let it grow.

41. Go to happy hour.

You have to make time to grow relationships. There is probably a group of people that head to happy hour on Friday from time to time. There may be optional celebratory get-togethers. People may have send-off parties for someone's retirement or job change. These are prime opportunities not only have a good time, but to meet people in your company you might otherwise never meet. It is a great way to reconnect with those you don't interact with all the time. In this atmosphere, you may gather knowledge on projects, uncover opportunities to collaborate, or even find a next step for yourself or someone on your team.

When you can, attend. I know it might take time away from family or personal interests, but attending optional social events has business value. Don't go crazy. If you don't drink, don't drink. That's not what this is about. If you do drink, drink in moderation. This may be optional, but these people still work where you work. Have a drink, mingle and make connections. They will come in handy back at the office.

Action

- Determine how often you are comfortable attending optional social gatherings. Consider once a quarter at a minimum.

- When attending, engage those you know to gain introductions to those you don't.

- Avoid asking "What do you do?" instead ask, "What's the most interesting thing happening in your world?"

42. Be an associate brand advocate.

Part of your job is to shine a spot light on the good works of your associates. Your associates are busy doing the work. Just like you need to redefine success to mean the success of your team, you must give credit where credit is due.

Speak up about the great things your associates are doing. In your one-on- ones with your leader, outline work efforts and specifically who is contributing and how. Provide updates on personal development. Tell your leader who you believe may someday take your place. Who is close to promotion?

When working with other leaders, pay special attention to their open positions. What skills make someone successful in that area of the business? Watch for natural next promotional steps for your associates. Make sure you highlight your associates' skills and mention what a career path could look like in the future.

Do not take credit for their work effort or even too much of their development. Being a brand advocate is not about you, it is about those that work for you. It is about taking pride in the success and development of your associates. A good leader reflects praise back to the team. This shows true leadership, respect and maturity. A leader who constantly takes credit loses the respect of their team and demonstrates no self-confidence.

Action

- For each associate, keep a list of work initiatives and development activity.

- Provide updates to your leader on a regular basis.

- Share successes with your peer group and other leaders in the organization.

43. Get them promoted.

You know all that work you did giving your people opportunities to stretch, being a brand advocate and talking about their career path? Well, it's about that time. When you know someone is ready for their next step, give them full support and build them up.

Typically, after someone has been in a position about two years, it is time to examine next steps. That's not to say someone can't promote after six months or stay in the same job 20 years, but consider what can happen in two years. The first year is really a learning year as an associate learns how to effectively execute their job. In the second year, a high potential associate will begin to perfect their work and stretch into more responsibilities. When you see an associate who's had a stellar second or third year, be ready to support their next step.

It will be hard for you and your team to see someone go. Losing good people is never easy, but losing them to a great opportunity for growth makes it a lot easier. It also gives you an opportunity to hire and develop someone and, in turn, develop yourself. Truly, the best measure of a leader is how well they develop, grow, and promote their associates.

Action

- Identify through one on one conversations when your associate is ready for their next step.

- Stay informed of openings in the company.

- When a decision to apply is finally made, be supportive by offering interview guidance, proof-reading resumes or portfolios and speaking with the hiring manager if appropriate.

- Even if your associate does not get the promotion, celebrate their bravery and identify what might be done next time.

44. Take a walk and say hello.

Business is about relationships. We talked about it over and over in this book. You need to grow those relationships; you need to meet new people. You need to care.

Be the person who says hello in the hall or on the elevator. If you have a large workplace, take a walk to other floors or building. Greet people. Ask people how they spend their day? Ask them what is the most interesting happening right now? Say hello to people you know and people you don't. Make an effort to know more people.

This is part of your personal brand. You should become the person that knows everyone. You know what they do, how you can help them and how they can help you. Even if it doesn't feel natural, you need to become the connector.

Action

- Always say hello to those you see on your way in and out of the office.

- Walk the floor or the building once per week to meet people.

- Keep a list of who you meet, what they do and how you might help them sometime in the future.

45. Use your peers.

Chances are you have a few leaders around you leading other teams. Your peers are those that are on a similar path and facing similar challenges. A good leader leverages available resources. This includes those around you who may possess expertise and strengths different than your own. Utilizing the leaders around you can help in a couple of ways.

First, your peers can serve as a great source of advice or a sounding board for new ideas. As a whole, your peer team provides a diverse background enabling you to see things from many different perspectives. By using this approach, you have a greater chance of developing a stronger strategy and uncovering pitfalls before they arise.

Leveraging your peers also shows a huge amount of trust, respect and team approach. Building this type of culture makes for a better place to work. You will enjoy work and your interactions and be more productive.

Finding the right was to leverage your peer team can prove challenging if a formal method is not developed. Create a Leadership Collaboration Council that brings your leadership peer group together bi-weekly. In this forum you and other leaders can present upcoming projects, host ideation sessions, ask for feedback, and have a roundtable. While no one wants another meeting, using this time wisely will enhance all leadership that attends.

Action

- Keep constant contact with your leadership peer group through:

    o Monthly one on one meetings

    o Formal collaboration venues

    o Informal discussions

- If no formal venue is used, talk with your leader and lead the charge for a Leadership Collaboration Council that would meet bi-weekly.

- Leverage leaders by asking for feedback and ideas to help evolve strategy and avoid pitfalls.

46. Don't forget to take time for you.

Leaders, especially new leaders trying to prove themselves, can forget something very basic. You have to take care of yourself. Late nights, early mornings, and fast food are not great habits to pick up. You may find yourself abandoning things you once made time for such as hobbies, fitness and friends. This can make your new leadership adventure a nightmare. You excelled to this position to have a better and happier life, don't fall into the trap that you can't still do that.

You have to step away, trust your team, and find time for you. First, consider your health. If you aren't doing some physical activity, you need to. I don't care what kind of shape you are in; you need to schedule time three times a week to do something active. Let this mentality extend to how you eat as well. It may be really easy to grab fast food all the time, but try to find better options. Choose healthier restaurants or selections. Take your lunch and really only splurge once a week or less.

Second, you need time to enjoy the things that bring you joy. That may be family time, a specific sport or some other hobby. Mark that time off so that you are purposely dedicating time to doing something you love. Taking time for this may feel selfish, but you deserve joy in your life. If you give these activities up you may end up resenting your job.

Lastly, don't neglect your friends and family. You don't work so hard to abandon your personal life. Purposely disconnect from work when you can and dedicate your attention to your family or friends. Have people over or go out on the town, but spend time with those that you care about and that build you up.

Action

- Schedule one hour, three times a week minimum for physical activity.

- Limit fast food to no more than once per week.

- Schedule weekly time dedicated to a specific hobby or activity that brings you joy.

- Disconnect from work and concentrate your attention on your family or friends.

- Plan one event per month at a minimum that places you in a social setting with people you care about such as a dinner party, movie date or a night out on the town.

47. Be humble.

To lead is an honor. Being arrogant and self-centered is a sure way to find yourself out of a job. You have been trusted with the wellbeing of people and a part of a company. You are valuable and deserving, but you must remain humble and appreciative.

It's true, the work you do is important. The work your team does is important. You are making a difference. You are contributing to the greater goal of you company. But you are not the only one making a difference. All of those around you are also valuable and contributing, some more and some less. If you didn't show up for work tomorrow, it would be difficult, but probably not impossible for your company to go on.

Don't get me wrong, I don't mean to belittle your contribution. I'm sure replacing you would not be easy. But remember, you want to be the person with whom people enjoy working. You want to be easy to work with, fun, and a high contributor. You want to be humble and build up those around you. You don't want to be an arrogant know-it-all; you want to be a confident contributor.

Action

- Take note of how you speak up in meetings and ask yourself:

    o Am I offering worthwhile information?

    o Am I listening to understand or respond?

    o If someone else was saying this, how would I feel?

- Make an effort to listen more than you talk.

- Show appreciation for those around you as they are helping you to your own success.

- Thank whatever higher power you choose for the things you have in your life.

48. Take pride and be proud in all you do.

I know we just talked about being humble. Definitely remain humble. But you must also be proud in the work accomplished while taking pride as you do the work.

First, take pride. Taking pride in what you do isn't about being arrogant or entitled. It's about understanding that what you do matters. Show pride by doing any work assigned to you the best way you know how. That means stepping up to plate when it comes to executing all work, not just the parts you enjoy. Bring pride when coaching, developing, and creating relationships that help you attain the goals in front of you.

Second, be proud. Be proud of how you contribute to the company. Be proud of your team. Be proud of who you are and how you show up to work every day. Remember, there are a lot of people counting on you. Your company, your team, and those you support all rely on you to one degree of another. Knowing you have the skills and abilities to meet the challenge is something of which you should be proud.

How, you ask? This may feel a little fluffy if you don't put tactics around it. And I did promise to provide actual things you can do. The key is to create tactics around the action of being prideful. You have to find a way to make sure you are bringing your "A" game all the time. You also have to take time and remind yourself of the important things you and your team have accomplished. This is a time to use the power of the list.

Action

- Create folder with multiple documents:

  o Create a Pride List for yourself, a list that captures things you've done this year of which you are proud.

  o Create a Pride List for each associate on your team – projects may overlap.

  o Create a Pride List for the team as a whole with larger efforts or cultural contributions.

- Be specific in your list entries. Include dates and details so as not to forget any pertinent information.

- Set a monthly reminder to review the lists in their entirety and add new items.

- In all work you do, ask yourself if you are doing the best you can. If not, take actions to change your approach like discussing with your leader or you mentor.

49. Challenge the norm.

We have talked about how you don't know it all a couple of times. While that is true, no one else knows it all either. That means the whole "we've always done it this way" doesn't fly. Part of what you can bring is some fresh thinking and new perspective. Consider your background and the lessons you have learned in your career. Chances are, something about you is unique and makes you an expert in the room. It's time to let that unique insight shine in the form of respectfully challenging the norm.

First, identify in your background what unique perspective you bring. What about your past experience makes your opinion an expert opinion? It might come from past work experience. It could have something do with your education. It could have something to do with your hobbies and interests. It might even be how or where you were raised. We are all different which makes us each uniquely equipped to bring a different perspective.

Second is to actually challenge the norm. This is a delicate concept. Bringing new ideas can be a bit of a balancing act. You may feel as though you are too young in your role to provide new ideas. You're not. You do, however need to balance respect for the history of the company and those that have been doing the work with how you bring new and innovative ideas. Ask questions to learn more. Don't dictate how things ought to be and don't bash the way things are.

People are passionate about processes they've created or ideas they've brought to life. Respect each person as a free-thinking contributor that you want to work alongside.

Actions

- Outline what makes you different. Include:

    o Work History

    o Education

    o Hobbies / Interests

    o Life Experiences

- Leverage these differences to examine current work processes, products, services etc.

- Ask yourself these questions:

    o Do I have an idea that can make this better?

    o Is this mine to change?

    o If not, can I make a respectful and collaborative recommendation without damaging the relationship?

50. Get ready for more.

This is only a step on your life path. What you do now will very likely not be what you do 10 years from now. You are a leader of people, it's true, but you are still being led. You are in a dual role of sorts. You are responsible to help your associates on their path, but you have to consider your own career path. I hope your leader is also your advocate, pushing you to develop and excel.

Prepare for your own next step. Find out what excites you, where you passion lies. Manage your own personal brand. Look for stretch opportunities for yourself. Continue to seek out professional development education. Have conversations about the future with your leader. Actively manage your career.

Someday, it will be time for you take your next step. If you are a strong culture leader, you will likely face a flood of emotions as you leave your team. There is never a good time to leave a position. There are projects left to do, work let to accomplish, people left to develop. If you are constantly waiting for the right time, you will be waiting forever.

But, if you are 100% ready to move, you've waited too long. A great leader once told me, when you are about 80% ready, start looking.

Action

- Look at the larger organization and make a list of functional areas and positions that may be appropriate for your next step.

- Continue development and education towards those areas.

- Have open and honest conversations with your leader to uncover areas of opportunities and to gain support.

- When a position becomes available, be ready to chase your passion and get that next step.

In Closing

I truly hope you have found this book useful. Like I said in the beginning, use what you can. Use what makes sense. Some of this may not apply to you, your industry or your company's culture. No two companies are the same. As a matter of fact, no two teams are the same. But, I hope that many of these tips are useful to you. And while not every person I've had the honor and privilege to lead may consider me the best leader they've ever had, I do hope each felt valued. I am a leader who truly cares.

The longer you lead, the more tips you will develop for yourself. It's not about being perfect. You aren't. You will make mistakes. You'll cancel one-on-ones, lead pointless meetings, and hurt people's feelings. Just do the best you can do, and do it better tomorrow.

In all that you've read, there are really three main categories in which all these tips fall.

Build yourself.

Build your team.

Build relationships.

Do these things and you and your team will grow and succeed. Lead Happier!

ABOUT THE AUTHOR

Stephen Jones grew up in Oklahoma and developed a love of leadership early in his career. In college, a part time job selling pagers (yes, pagers) at a local mall spawned a career of nearly two decades in the wireless industry. Stephen has provided leadership and strategic direction in Sales, Marketing and Operations. He continues to lead teams to success.

Stephen currently resides in Park ridge, IL, with his wife and children where he enjoys local community and neighborhood events, live music, Chicago sports and his children's numerous activities.

Stephen is currently developing an online resource and community for leaders to share and connect at: www.leadhappier.com